Original title:

The Starfish Story

Editor: Jessica Elisabeth Luik

Author: Sebastian Sarapuu

ISBN HARDBACK: 978-9916-86-427-2

ISBN PAPERBACK: 978-9916-86-428-9

Tides of Compassion

Waves of kindness, softly swelling,
Hug the shore in silent grace.
Moonlit beams, a tale foretelling,
Of hearts at peace, forever trace.

Whispers through the salty breeze,
Bind the world in tender care.
Oceans speak in fluent ease,
Love and hope, beyond compare.

Foamy crests, their stories weave,
Blanket lives that gently sleep.
Through the night, we too believe,
In the tides, our spirits keep.

Rippled Benevolence

Gentle waters, softly part,
Echoes of a giving heart.
In each ripple, stories told,
Acts of kindness, bright and bold.

Sunlit streams caress the land,
Grains of hope fall from the hand.
Infinite, the waves extend,
Showing love that has no end.

Benevolence in liquid form,
Crafts the calm amidst the storm.
In the quiet, truths unfold,
Empathy, a force untold.

Hands in the Sand

Fingers trace the grains of time,
Woven tales in simple lines.
Moments fleeting, yet so grand,
Lives entwined, hands in the sand.

Footprints fade but whispers stay,
Echoes of another day.
By the sea, where dreams expand,
Hearts unite, hands in the sand.

Golden light of evening's kiss,
Seals the day in perfect bliss.
Memories like castles stand,
Built with love, hands in the sand.

Episodes of an Ocean Heart

Every wave, a story told,
In the depths, the secrets hold.
Chapters written by the sea,
Echo in eternity.

Wistful breezes paint the air,
Tales of love and deep despair.
Currents pull and gently start,
Episodes of an ocean heart.

Foamy whispers kiss the shore,
Silent oaths forevermore.
Waves depart yet leave a mark,
In the soul, their subtle spark.

Where the Waves Break

Where the waves break on rugged shore,
Secrets spoken by the sea.
Foam fades away with tales of yore,
Whispered from eternity.

Nautical dreams in each retreat,
Glimmer under twilight's veil.
Sand and stone in silence meet,
The cadence of a sailor's tale.

Horizon's blaze, the morning wakes,
Every dawn reborn anew.
The heart answers as the wave breaks,
Embracing skies of sunlit blue.

Hands of the Tide

Hands of the tide, in softest hold,
Cradle secrets, deep and old.
Mysteries in waters bold,
Whispered lore yet to be told.

They mold the shore in ceaseless dance,
Caressing sands in reticent glance.
In moonlit glow, they find romance,
Weaving myths that time enchants.

Ever moving, with strength and grace,
Sculpting Earth's eternal face.
Hands of the tide, they interlace,
Leaving marks in every place.

Compassionate Currents

Compassionate currents weave and wander,
Through marine realms, they softly ponder.
Embrace the reefs, in loving slumber,
Bearing kindness in their number.

Currents whisper, gently guide,
Through ocean's heart, they quietly slide.
Bringing life where they reside,
In every ebb and steady tide.

They caress, they nurture, unseen care,
In water's realm, so vast, so fair.
Life's cradle in waves laid bare,
Compassion flows in ocean's air.

Ocean's Silent Rescue

Ocean's silent rescue, deep and quiet,
Beneath the waves, the storm is mild.
In the depths, no man-made riot,
Just the solace of nature's child.

It soothes the souls stranded at sea,
Gentle pulses cradle their plea.
In nights deepest tranquility,
Ocean's calm sets the spirit free.

Lighthouse beams in the distant night,
Guiding lost back to the light.
In silent depths, hearts reunite,
Find safe harbor, from endless flight.

The Savior by the Sea

Where waves and winds in union dance,
A lighthouse stands with steadfast glance,
It guards the sailors lost in night,
Its beacon brings them home to light.

The storm may rage, the sea may roar,
But still it shines forevermore,
A symbol of hope in the darkest hour,
Guiding ships through nature's power.

Alone it stands on rugged shore,
A sentinel forevermore,
Its light a savior, near and far,
A guiding, constant, northern star.

Pebbles of Promise

On tranquil sands where shorelines meet,
Lie pebbles small beneath our feet,
Each holds a story, timeless, vast,
Fragments of a distant past.

They whisper secrets of the deep,
Of oceans wide and ancient sleep,
Polished smooth by time and tide,
In them, the world's great truths reside.

Collect them close, these gems so rare,
For in their silence, dreams they bear,
Promise etched in every line,
A bridge to worlds that intertwine.

Bringers of Brilliance

In skies where twilight fades to glow,
Appears a dance that crescents know,
Stars awaken, one by one,
To herald night as day is done.

With sparkling eyes, they pierce the veil,
Of mysteries that stars entail,
Ancient light from distant past,
Their brilliance for our souls to cast.

They map the heavens, guide our way,
In guardian brilliance till break of day,
Silent keepers of the lore,
Bringers of dreams and so much more.

Songs of the Shoal

Beneath the waves where light plays soft,
Lie secrets lost and currents aloft,
A symphony of whispered tones,
In watery depths, where life abounds.

The dolphins sing in joyous leap,
While mermaids in their caves do keep,
Melodies that ebb with grace,
In the ocean's vast, embracing space.

We listen close, and hear the song,
Of life within, so pure and strong,
A testament to sea's own soul,
The boundless, timeless, living shoal.

Tides of Tenderness

Whispers ride the twilight breeze,
Soft as morning's gentle light.
Waves of kindness, never cease,
Dancing through the endless night.

Hearts entwined in moonlit seas,
Anchored deep, unseen delight.
Love's embrace, a warm release,
Lifting souls to soaring height.

In the ebb and flow of dreams,
Tender tides hold secrets tight.
Echoes of eternity,
Guided by the stars' dim light.

Through the storms and quiet streams,
Steadfast, true, compassion's might.
Binding hearts with silver beams,
In this ocean of the night.

With each turn and rise, belief,
In these waters pure and bright.
Tides of tenderness, relief,
Carry us till morning light.

On the Shore of Mercy

Glimmers of a dawn yet born,
Cast in hues of hope and grace.
Where the waves meet sands well-worn,
Mercy's touch leaves not a trace.

Footprints washed by time's embrace,
Stories lost, yet memories stay.
Trials faced with stoic face,
On this shore at break of day.

Hands that reach to lift the low,
In the tide's unending flow.
Compassion, like the winds, will blow,
Healing all who bend and bow.

Gentle whispers, soft and slow,
Speak of love's enduring glow.
From the depths where angels tow,
Mercy's light begins to grow.

Upon this shore, where hearts renew,
In the sand, a sacred vow.
With each wave, our spirits grew,
Mercy's touch, we here endow.

Salvation Sands

Golden shores where dreams unfold,
Beneath a sky of gathered wings.
Stories in the grains retold,
Of peace and hope that always sings.

Footsteps venturing ever bold,
Leave behind the past life brings.
In the sands, a love so old,
Binding hearts with timeless strings.

Waters cleanse what's yet unseen,
Washing sorrow to the sea.
In this place, our spirits glean,
Glimpses of what ought to be.

Salvation sought in desert's gleam,
Found within this sacred lea.
On these sands, we find the beam,
Of a love that sets us free.

No more the shadows haunt our way,
In the light of mercy's hand.
Here we find the dawn of day,
In the soil of salvation sands.

Intertidal Dreams

Between the ebb and flow of tides,
Where ocean whispers secrets low,
The moon's soft light in darkness hides,
And dreams begin to ebb and grow.

Shells and stones are stories spun,
In patterns left upon the shore,
The intertidal dance begun,
As waves retreat and then restore.

Footprints vanish, lives concealed,
In sands that hold the world's lament,
Beneath the surface, truths revealed,
In symphonies of water bent.

Beneath the stars, the sea does gleam,
A canvas wide for night's embrace,
In silent waves, we catch a dream,
From ocean's heart, a dream to chase.

Twilight Guardians

As day departs and shadows cast,
The twilight guardians awake,
Their silent watch until the last,
To guard the night and daybreak.

In trees and skies, a solace found,
Amongst the stars, their vigil keep,
Their realms of light and dark unbound,
For them, the night is never deep.

They whisper in the evening breeze,
A language old as time and space,
From moonlit meadows to the seas,
They hold the world's most sacred place.

With wings of silver, eyes of flame,
They roam the twilight's vast domain,
Forever tied to dawn's soft claim,
Their watch eternal, they remain.

Harbingers of Hope

In darkest hours, silent cries,
For harbingers of hope appear,
With wings of dawn and unseen ties,
They dry the mourner's every tear.

They come with whispers in the night,
A promise carried on the breeze,
Guiding lost souls towards the light,
Amidst the sighs of bending trees.

From fields of sorrow, dreams revive,
Where shattered hearts begin to mend,
In fragile moments, they arrive,
To signal love that knows no end.

Their presence felt but rarely seen,
A gentle nudge to find our way,
Within their grace, the soul is clean,
And hope returns to light the day.

The Star-Keeper

Amid the vast celestial sea,
The star-keeper with care does tread,
With lantern bright and spirit free,
He guides the stars above our head.

His hands have touched the very night,
To set each glowing gem alight,
In constellations, patterns tight,
He weaves a tale of endless flight.

The galaxies, his canvas grand,
A masterpiece of cosmic blend,
In boundless realms, he takes his stand,
To cradle stars that never end.

In silence deep, his vigil kept,
A guardian of dreams untold,
Where wishes softly, gently crept,
Into the night, through ages old.

Ebb and Flow of Caring

In the cycle of the sea,
Waves rise and gently fall.
Hearts beat in harmony,
Responding to love's call.

In moments, we are strong,
In others, we are weak.
Yet care, a boundless song,
Is what our spirits seek.

Stretched out by the shore,
Ocean's breath, a soothing touch.
Love's whisper says there's more,
In tides, we find so much.

Flowing with the moon,
Our souls, they ebb and flow.
A dance beneath the dune,
In unity, we grow.

The ocean holds us tight,
In its arms, we sway.
With caring as our light,
We guide each other's way.

One Star at a Time

In night's vast, endless dome,
One star begins to shine.
It guides the weary home,
A beacon through the time.

Each star, a story told,
Of dreams that dare to gleam.
In skies of midnight gold,
They brighten every dream.

Together, stars align,
To weave a cosmic tale.
Their light, a steady sign,
That hope shall never fail.

Through darkness, they persist,
In silence, yet so bright.
In every star, a wish,
A promise held in light.

As we gaze up above,
The universe's chime.
We find, in stars, our love,
One sparkle at a time.

Tales of the Tidepools

Beside the ocean's edge,
Tiny worlds we find.
In each rocky wedge,
Life's mysteries unwind.

Crabs scuttle side to side,
In pools, they safely hide.
Where secrets do abide,
As tidal waters bide.

Anemones in bloom,
Their tentacles unfurl.
In every shadowed room,
A story they will twirl.

Where sea stars slowly roam,
Their colors bold and bright.
In tidepools, they find home,
Beneath the moon's soft light.

Each tide brings new reveal,
A chapter fresh and rare.
In tidepools, we can feel,
The ocean's loving care.

Lives Among the Seafoam

Upon the sandy shore,
Where seafoam dances free,
The ocean whispers more,
Of lives in harmony.

Seagulls call in flight,
Their songs, a coastal tome.
With waves, they greet the light,
Lives gathered in seafoam.

Driftwood tells a tale,
Of journeys long and wide.
Each piece a fragile sail,
On life's unending tide.

Algae softly sways,
A dance beneath the blue.
In swirls of ocean haze,
New lives are born anew.

Among the foamy crest,
We too, our stories weave.
In nature's gentle nest,
Our hearts, we leave, believe.

Shores of a Gentle Heart

Upon the shores of a gentle heart,
Soft waves of love, they never part.
Whispers blend with ocean's hue,
In silent embrace, thoughts imbue.

Footprints linger on golden sand,
Traced by fate's unerring hand.
Winds weave stories, old and new,
A tapestry of dreams anew.

Seashell secrets, fragments of time,
Echo memories in perfect rhyme.
Seagulls dance above the blue,
In the gentle heart, love renews.

Moonlit nights, a silver glow,
Illuminating the paths we know.
Heartbeats sync with ocean's art,
On the shores of a gentle heart.

Waves serenade, a soulful plea,
A symphony of love set free.
On these shores, where dreams impart,
Lives the essence of a gentle heart.

Rescuing Tides

When darkness falls and shadows creep,
The tides arise from ocean deep.
With courage bold, they gently stride,
To rescue dreams the world denied.

Each wave a promise, strong and true,
Of brighter days and skies of blue.
In tidal dance, they lift the soul,
Mending hearts to make them whole.

Against the storm, they fiercely stand,
Washing fears from drifting sand.
Hope restored in their embrace,
Infinite grace on their face.

Tides of change, they come and go,
Carrying love on undertow.
With every crest, a lullaby,
Guide us where our spirits fly.

The moon commands their ebb and flow,
In tidal strength, our hearts bestow.
Rescuing tides of time and space,
In their arms, we find our place.

Echoes Beneath the Waves

Beneath the waves, where silence reigns,
Echoes whisper through sea's veins.
Ancient songs of time, they weave,
Mysteries that oceans leave.

In depths where shadows softly glide,
Secrets in the currents ride.
Fathomless and dark they keep,
The dreams that in the waters sleep.

Corals grow in colors bright,
Amid the depths of blue twilight.
Their whispers twine in liquid flow,
In the underwater glow.

Echoes of the ocean's past,
Eternally they flow and cast.
Ghostly tales of sunken ships,
In the deep where the silence skips.

Submerged worlds where memories hide,
In the vast, unending tide.
Listen close to what sea gave:
The echoes beneath the waves.

Whispers in the Tide

Whispers travel with the tide,
Softly spoken, deftly guide.
Stories told in liquid prose,
Where the restless ocean flows.

They carry wishes far and near,
Words of comfort, love, and cheer.
Each soft murmur, waves convey,
Messages to light the way.

In the hush of twilight's gray,
Seabreezes launch dreams to play.
Carried on the salt-kissed breeze,
Whispers float with utmost ease.

Hearts attuned to ocean's song,
Find solace where they once belonged.
In the rhythm, whispers blend,
Promising that hearts will mend.

Tide speaks softly, do not fear,
For every whisper, we will hear.
In the dance of time and sea,
Whispers guide to destiny.

Waves of a Single Hope

In the deep blue, whispers glide,
Under the moon, dreams reside.
Foam and tides in endless scope,
Merge in waves of a single hope.

Golden light on rippling crest,
Sunset hues in ocean's rest.
Harmony in rhythmic rope,
Held by waves of a single hope.

Hearts aflight on breezes soft,
Chasing stars that shine aloft.
Drawn to shores where spirits cope,
On the waves of a single hope.

Footprints fade on shifting sands,
Written tales of distant lands.
To the horizon, we elope,
Guided by waves of a single hope.

Sand and Salvation

Grains of gold beneath our feet,
Silent songs the sands repeat.
Paths we walk in sacred trust,
Sand and salvation, fair and just.

Footprints trace where dreams unfold,
Stories ancient, secrets told.
Time and tide in cosmic thrust,
Held by sand and salvation's dust.

Winds caress the desert's grace,
Shaping dunes in slow embrace.
We with wonder, no mistrust,
Follow the sand to salvation's gust.

Twilight shadows calm the land,
Waves retreat at night's command.
In this vast expanse, adjust,
Faith found in sand and salvation's crust.

Beachcomber's Mission

Morning mist on quiet beach,
Treasures lie within our reach.
Shells and secrets, waves unleash,
On the beachcomber's mission speech.

Tidal whispers call us near,
Horizon bright, sky so clear.
Each new find a boundless cheer,
On a mission, we persevere.

Driftwood tales in hands so worn,
Fragments of a dream reborn.
Guided by the ocean's horn,
Seek the mission sworn and sworn.

Glistening under the pale moon,
Echoes of an ancient tune.
Step by step, beneath the dune,
On the beachcomber's mission, soon.

Celestial Creatures of the Shore

Starlit waves on sandy coast,
Guardians of the night at most.
Celestial creatures, silent boast,
Of secrets in the ocean host.

Moonbeams dance in tidal pools,
Myths and legends, ocean's tools.
Mysteries are timeless fuels,
For celestial creatures' schools.

Glow of dusk and bright sun's rise,
Reveals wonders to our eyes.
Upon the shore where magic lies,
Celestial creatures, no disguise.

Waves resound in cosmic song,
Where these beings all belong.
In this realm where nights are long,
Celestial creatures, pure and strong.

Waves of the Altruist

A hand that reaches far and wide,
For love that surges like the tide,
In every heart, a beam of light,
Guiding us through darkest night.

Selfless acts, like oceans vast,
Kindness flows, a bridge to cast,
To lift and buoy a soul adrift,
From waters deep, we find the lift.

With every wave, the joy we share,
Ripples forth into the air,
Cascading through the lives we meet,
On every shore, a kind heart beats.

Through tempests fierce and tranquil seas,
Altruism sways with ease,
In every drop, a world of care,
In giving more, we're always there.

Eternal waves that never cease,
Bringing warmth and fostering peace,
The altruist, like tide so true,
Forever flows, from me to you.

Seashore Guardians

Along the edge where land meets sea,
My faithful friends, you stand with me,
With silent vigil, ever keep,
The secrets that the oceans reap.

Sentinels of sand and stone,
And driftwood sculptures, time has honed,
You guard the coast with steadfast might,
Through day's bright sun and moonlit night.

The waves become your whispered voice,
In every splash, a subtle choice,
To tell the tales of ancient lore,
And guide the wanderers to shore.

With footprints left on shifting sands,
You write the stories of these lands,
Where every breeze and salty air,
Reminds us of your watchful care.

So here we'll stand as one with you,
Seashore guardians, hearts so true,
Together through the rise and fall,
United by the ocean's call.

Ocean's Gentle Breath

Through gentle waves and tranquil streams,
The ocean breathes in silent dreams,
Whispering secrets, tales untold,
In currents warm and waters cold.

Each sigh and swell, a calming balm,
The ocean's breath, forever calm,
Upon the shore where whispers lay,
In soft embrace at break of day.

From depths unknown and distant shores,
The ocean's breath forever roars,
A symphony of life and grace,
In every tide and every trace.

With every ebb and flow it shows,
A dance of life, a knowing prose,
Unfolding mysteries in its path,
The gentle breath of ocean's wrath.

So let us breathe this tranquil air,
And find the peace that lingers there,
In rhythmic pulses, day and night,
The ocean's breath, our heart's delight.

Twilight's Gentle Embrace

As day fades to a golden hue,
The sky transforms, a twilight view,
In gentle whispers of the breeze,
An evening calm as hearts find ease.

The stars awake in velvet skies,
A lullaby that softly sighs,
With every twinkle, dreams ignite,
In twilight's tender, soft embrace.

The shadows stretch and night unfolds,
In shades of silver, bronze, and gold,
A tranquil peace that night bestows,
Upon the world in quiet rows.

Beneath the moon's enchanting light,
The world bathes in a calm so bright,
Each star a beacon in the night,
Guiding us with gentle might.

And as we drift to slumber's gate,
In dreams we'll find our destined fate,
Held close within the night's sweet grace,
In twilight's gentle, warm embrace.

Heartprints in the Sand

Beneath the sky, our toes did dance,
Whispers shared in sweet romance;
Tides may rise, years may flow,
Yet heartprints in the sand will show.

Laughter echoed, waves did play,
Stars adorned the twilight's stay;
In every grain, our memories stand,
Imprinted deep upon the sand.

Moonlit nights and sunny dawns,
Love eternal, ever drawn;
As waters kiss the golden strand,
Heartprints linger in the land.

Silent vows beneath the sea,
Secrets kept eternally;
With each tide's gentle command,
Our love's marks remain in sand.

Ebbing tides and shifting hues,
Bound by memories, love renews;
In every footprint, hand in hand,
Heartprints mark our love's command.

Marina Mercy

Quiet waters, tranquil hue,
Marina's grace, the sky's deep blue;
Boats that hum a gentle song,
In mercy's arms, we drift along.

Sunset's gold, horizons wide,
Soft waves lap at evening's tide;
Harbor safe from tempests' scorn,
Here mercy's touch, we're reformed.

Lighthouse beacons guide the way,
Silence wraps the close of day;
Stars emerge, a twinkling choir,
Marina mercy to admire.

Ocean's breath on windswept sails,
Softly, softly, tell their tales;
In the stillness, peace unfurls,
Mercy's calm in boundless swirls.

Anchored here, the heart finds rest,
Cradled in the sea's caress;
In marina's gentle sway,
Mercy keeps the storms at bay.

Galactic Gratitude

Stardust trails across the night,
Gratitude in celestial light;
Planets, moons, and comets gleam,
Universal thanks, supreme.

Milky Way, an endless stream,
Grains of time in vast esteem;
Cosmic wonders, journeys far,
Gratitude in every star.

Nebulas with colors bright,
Gifts of awe in silent flight;
Galaxies in endless queue,
Thankful for the cosmic view.

Orbiting this sphere of blue,
Grateful for the life in view;
Constellations, wise and old,
Teach us tales yet to be told.

In the darkest space, profound,
Gratitude in silence found;
Through the universe we glide,
Thankful for this wondrous ride.

Sands of Solace

In the dunes of life's embrace,
Finding comfort, finding grace;
Every footprint, gentle trace,
Sands of solace, time's soft pace.

Golden grains beneath our feet,
Silent prayers in rhythms sweet;
With each step, our worries fleet,
Solace found in calm retreat.

Desert winds, a song so mild,
Nature's voice, serene and wild;
In this land, our hearts compile,
All the peace within its aisle.

Twilight's glow on sands of gold,
Stories of the past retold;
In this quiet, we enfold,
Solace in the light we hold.

Lay us down, our spirits rest,
Here amidst the sands we're blessed;
In this haven, hearts confessed,
Solace in the endless quest.

Whispers of the Tidal Flats

The moonlight kisses dewy sand,
Where tidal whispers softly land,
Each ripple tells a secret tale,
As night unveils the ocean's veil.

Crabs scuttle in their dim ballet,
Starfish rest from light of day,
In shadows deep, where dreams abide,
Nature's whispers softly guide.

Shells collect the whispered lore,
Etched by waves upon the shore,
The flats sing songs of ebb and flow,
In moon's embrace, their secrets show.

Seabirds hush their daytime cries,
Underneath the starlit skies,
Each whisper woven in the breeze,
Sings of ancient, hidden seas.

The tidal flats, a quiet realm,
Nature's whispers at the helm,
In soft caress, the night renews,
Eternal dance of moonlit hues.

An Ocean's Gentle Hand

A touch so soft, a wave's caress,
Upon the shore in gentle press,
The ocean's hand, a calming balm,
Its whispers weave a soothing psalm.

Pebbles kissed by salty spray,
Carried by the tide's ballet,
Each motion speaks in tender grace,
An ocean's love in vast embrace.

Silver fish in moonlit trance,
Glide within the water's dance,
Reflections of a sky's deep blue,
In depths, the secrets gently strew.

Kelp forests sway in rhythmic cheer,
Echoing songs we bend to hear,
Their tendrils brush the sandy bed,
Caressing life that's ocean-bred.

The hand that shapes the rocky coast,
Bestows its gifts in silent boast,
With every wave, a tale is spun,
Of ancient times and days begun.

Among the Tide

To walk along the shifting sands,
With tide and time at my command,
Is to breathe a life renewed,
Among the ebb and flow's prelude.

Snails inch slowly past my feet,
In their shells, a world complete,
The tide tells tales of distant shores,
Of hidden depths and mystic lores.

The sun dips low, a scarlet blaze,
Reflections dance in twilight's haze,
Among the tide, the world seems stilled,
As if by dreams and wonder filled.

Seaweed strands like fingers trace,
Patterns in the ocean's grace,
Each tide anew delivers gifts,
In rhythmic dance, the spirit lifts.

Footprints washed away in brine,
Mark the passing sands of time,
Among the tide, I'm free to roam,
The ocean's edge, my transient home.

Sunset Resurrections

At dusk the sky ignites in flame,
A canvas painted without name,
The sea reflects the fiery glow,
In sunset's arms, the night will grow.

Birds return to shores they know,
Silhouettes in evening's show,
Their calls a chorus to the skies,
As day in somber pastel dies.

Each wave becomes a fleeting kiss,
A moment stolen into bliss,
As sunset breathes its warm caress,
Time renews in bold finesse.

The horizon drinks the molten gold,
Night's embrace begins to hold,
In twilight's gentle resurrection,
The world awaits in hushed reflection.

Stars emerge to take their place,
Draped upon the sky's vast lace,
In every sunset, life's redesigns,
A resurrection of twilight signs.

Beyond the Breakers

In moonlit whispers, oceans sigh,
A dance unseen by mortal eye.
Stars align with tales untold,
Waves embrace in their embrace, bold.

Voices echo from the deep,
Secrets ancient currents keep.
Through the mist, a lantern gleams,
Guiding souls by watery dreams.

Fathoms call with siren's song,
Heralds of a world where hearts belong.
Beyond breakers' crashing might,
Lies a realm of endless night.

Silent whispers, tempest winds,
Where love is bound, and life begins.
Surging tides, uncharted ways,
Whisper dreams through twilight haze.

Eternal voyage, drifting far,
Navigating by a northern star.
Beyond those breakers wild and free,
Lies the heart of mystery.

Rhythms of Renewal

Morning dew on fragile leaves,
Whispers of what the heart believes.
Sunlight dances, shadows fade,
Promises in the dawn conveyed.

Echoes of an ancient song,
Through the wind, it floats along.
Nature's cadence, wise and true,
Breathing life to all we knew.

Seeds of hope in fertile ground,
In silent sleep, their dreams are bound.
Awakened by the spring's first rain,
New beginnings rise again.

Cycles turn and time evolves,
As mystery of life resolves.
With each end, a fresh start blooms,
Renewal in the quiet rooms.

Hearts align with nature's pace,
In the dance of time and space.
Eternal rhythm, ever new,
Renewal's grace in all we do.

Ripples of Compassion

In quiet corners, kindness dwells,
Softly spoken, story tells.
A touch, a smile, a heartfelt deed,
A simple act, a broken need.

Compassion's ripples, ever wide,
Reaching hearts on every tide.
Where tears and laughter intertwine,
A binding force, scent divine.

Through tumult and the darkest night,
A beacon shines, a gentle light.
Hands extended, hearts embrace,
In unity, we find our place.

The world, a mirror of our care,
An echo of the love we share.
Boundless, infinite as space,
Rippling through the human race.

Each small gesture, a mighty wave,
Courage found, the unknown brave.
In every smile, compassion flows,
A river broad where understanding grows.

Beachcomber's Duty

Morning light on sandy shore,
A treasure hunt that forever more.
Each footprint left, a story told,
Among the shells and bits of gold.

A beachcomber's duty, day by day,
To seek the gems the tides convey.
To find the lost, the overlooked,
In nature's pages, deeply booked.

From driftwood tales to glassy finds,
A solace for the wandering minds.
Eons captured, stories old,
Secrets in the sea's fold.

Patients in the searching game,
Lulled by waves that call our name.
Collecting fragments, humbly so,
In the ebb and flow, we grow.

An endless quest, this sandy rite,
From morning's glow to evening light.
A Beachcomber, always true,
Guardians of the ocean's clue.

Saltwater Mercy

Beneath the azure, waves do unfold,
A whisper of mercy in oceans old,
Caressing shores with a gentle sigh,
Echoes of dreams beneath the sky.

In salt-kissed winds, a tale is spun,
Of solace found where blueness runs,
A healing touch in each tide's sweep,
Promises kept in waters deep.

Foam-laced edges, secrets they guard,
Merciful tides on beaches charred,
A dance of currents, calm yet free,
Saltwater's mercy, eternally.

By moonlight's grace and sun's bright gleam,
Rivers of hope in streams that dream,
From crest to trough, a soothing song,
The ocean's mercy, everlong.

And where the sea meets the horizon's crest,
A tranquil heart finds peaceful rest,
In every swell and wave-born plea,
Saltwater mercy sets souls free.

Lighthouse Benevolence

Amid the tempest, standing tall,
A beacon bright, guiding all,
Its light a promise through the dark,
A realm of hope, a steadfast spark.

Waves collide and winds may thrash,
But through the night, a gentle flash,
Guardian of sailors, lost and cold,
Benevolence in towers bold.

In mist and fog, the light remains,
A guiding hand through tempest's chains,
Harbor whispers to weary hearts,
Of safety where the journey starts.

A symbol stolid, against harsh gales,
Benevolence behind each sail,
Its glow, a promise to the far,
Leading ships with hope's bright star.

Night retreats as dawn draws near,
Lighthouse benevolence calms each fear,
In light's embrace, all worries cease,
A sentinel of mercy and peace.

Sea's Kind Whisper

Upon the shore where dreams alight,
The sea's kind whisper through the night,
A melody of waves' soft crest,
Lulls weary hearts to gentle rest.

Silvered glow on ocean's face,
Dances with the dawn's warm grace,
Singing lullabies to morning dew,
A timeless song both old and new.

Foam-tipped fingers reach the sand,
In quiet hushes, hand in hand,
Each wave a verse, each splash a rhyme,
Marked gently by the passing time.

In every ripple, secrets told,
Of kindness in the ocean's hold,
The whispering sea with stories kind,
Touching the heart, soothing the mind.

Beneath the sky's expansive dome,
The sea's kind whisper calls you home,
A tender note, a loving plea,
Infinity in tranquility.

Coastal Reflection

At water's edge where thoughts run deep,
Reflections in the waves that sweep,
A mirror of the soul displayed,
In coastal whispers, secrets laid.

The sunshine writes upon the sea,
Each ripple pens a memory,
Of joys and sorrows interweaved,
In tidal tales, our hearts believed.

Between the grains of sunlit sand,
Whispers of past in nature's hand,
Each footprint tells a fleeting tale,
As breezes fill the sails that sail.

A stretch of shore, a moment's pause,
To ponder life and all its laws,
In silent waves, reflections cast,
Of futures dreamt and anchors past.

So stand and gaze, let worries drift,
In coastal reflection, find your gift,
The ebb and flow, life's great design,
On shores of time, our paths align.

Sand and Salvation

In the desert, dreams are spun,
Underneath the blazing sun,
Mirages dance with every dawn,
Hope persists, though strength is gone.

Grains of sand, so infinite,
Test the will with every bit,
Yet within this sea of gold,
Lies a story, yet untold.

Beneath the scorching sky's embrace,
Footprints fade without a trace,
But a journey's worth is found,
In the silence, in the ground.

Cacti stand as sentinels,
Guarding secrets, farewells,
Every dune a challenge met,
Every step a noble bet.

From this barren, harsh terrain,
Life anew will rise again,
Sand and salvation intertwined,
A testament to spirit, blind.

Ocean's Whispered Hopes

Waves cascade with gentle grace,
Secrets hidden in their trace,
Whispers of the past reside,
In the ocean's ebbing tide.

Foam caresses jagged rocks,
Soothing all that time unlocks,
Stories told in subtle sweeps,
Beneath the surface, silence keeps.

Moonlight glistens on the crest,
Dreams of sailors put to rest,
In the lull of night's embrace,
Hopes find solace, interlace.

Currents drift with quiet might,
Pulling hearts from darkest night,
Promise holds in every hue,
Ocean's depths, a gentle cue.

Through the mist of morning dew,
Hope emerges, clear and true,
Whispered waves and tranquil brine,
Hearts and sea, forever bind.

One Shoreline at a Time

Every wave that meets the sand,
Shapes the dreams we gently planned,
In the rhythm of the sea,
Find our place, our destiny.

Footprints mark the winding path,
Moments forged, for time to grasp,
Waves erase, but never steal,
Memories we deeply feel.

Sunset paints the sky with gold,
Stories of the day, retold,
In the hush of twilight's air,
Promises are laid out bare.

Seagulls cry, a mournful tune,
Underneath the silver moon,
In the dance of stars above,
Find our solace, find our love.

One shoreline at a time we tread,
With each heartbeat, words unsaid,
In the waves, we find our rhyme,
Oceans stretch, beyond our time.

Waves of Kindness

Acts of kindness, small and wide,
Flow like waves, with gentle tide,
In the ocean of despair,
Compassion lingers, love we share.

From each ripple, greatness grows,
In the hearts where kindness flows,
Every gesture, every smile,
Carries hope for many miles.

Sea of troubles, though we face,
Kindness brings a warm embrace,
In the depths of darkest night,
Tender deeds ignite the light.

Hands extended, oceans part,
Healing starts within the heart,
Like the waves that kiss the shore,
Kindness echoes, evermore.

Waves of kindness, boundless, free,
Shape a world where we can be,
In this vast and endless sea,
Kindness brings eternity.

Beneath the Azure Tides

Beneath the azure tides they sway,
In rhythms soft, the corals play.
Whispers of the deep-end's heart,
Guiding ships from drifting far.

Moonlight dances on the foam,
Seagulls guard the ocean's home.
Stars align and serve as guide,
To mariners on this endless tide.

Waves that sing a lullaby,
Mirrors to the boundless sky.
Time stands still in liquid grace,
With tales of old etched on its face.

Secrets of the sea unfold,
Stories of explorers bold.
In the deeps where shadows roam,
Breaths of life find their home.

Treasures hidden far below,
Mysteries the depths bestow.
Within the azure tides we see,
The ocean's endless memory.

Hope in a Handful

In a handful of ancient soil,
Lie dreams nurtured by the toil.
Seeds of hope, small and bright,
Take to root, and reach for light.

From the earth, a sprout will rise,
Stretching toward the morning skies.
With each leaf, a story told,
Of resilience, green and bold.

Raindrops whisper, sunbeams cheer,
Fragile sprout, do not fear.
Within each bud, a promise lies,
To bloom beneath the blue-touched skies.

Roots entwined in silent growth,
A silent pact, an earnest oath.
Through storm and drought, stay resolved,
Nature's song, life's mystery solved.

In this earth, our hopes combined,
In seeds of life, our futures twined.
Hope in hands, a simple creed,
Nurturing every tender seed.

Heartbeats by the Sea

Waves caress the sandy shore,
Whispering secrets evermore.
Heartbeats match the ocean's song,
Where souls and sea belong.

As the tide begins to rise,
Salt and wind, eternal ties.
Feet imprint the wet, cool land,
Nature's touch, a gentle hand.

Breaths of sea breeze fill the air,
Chasing worries, easing care.
In each heartbeat, life's embrace,
In each wave, we find our place.

Stars reflected, night so deep,
Seaward dreams, in silence keep.
Moonlight weaves its silver thread,
Connecting hearts, where spirits tread.

Heartbeats by the sea aligned,
With the rhythm, find comfort kind.
In the ebb and flow, we find,
The dance of life, calm and blind.

Morning's Gentle Resolve

Morning's light, so soft and new,
Kisses fields of glistening dew.
Whispers of a day reborn,
Grace the world in early morn.

Sunrise weaves with golden thread,
Promises of what's ahead.
Birdsongs blend in harmonies,
Floating on the morning breeze.

Dawn reflects on waters clear,
Brushing off the twilight's fear.
In this quiet, moments pause,
Nature's calm, without a clause.

Shadows fade with every ray,
Hope renews at break of day.
Through the veil, the truth we see,
Morning's gentle guarantee.

Graceful dawn, the world awakes,
Through morning's light, a journey makes.
With resolve, we greet the day,
In soft light, find our way.

Morning's Graceful Reach

The dawn breaks with golden hue,
Whispers of dreams turning true,
Soft light dances on the stream,
Morning awakens like a dream.

Birds sing in harmony's cast,
Night's shadows fading fast,
Leaves shimmer with the breeze,
Nature's whispers put you at ease.

Sunflower fields greet the day,
Bathed in dawn's gentle ray,
Petals unfold with the light,
A serene start, pure and bright.

Cool air kissing cheeks so sweet,
Dewdrops shimmering at your feet,
Gentle waves upon the shore,
Morning's grace, forever more.

Mountains bask in day's embrace,
Valleys greet the morning's grace,
Time moves with gentle ease,
Life begins anew, a perfect peace.

Heartstrings of the Sea

Ocean's whisper calls my name,
Heartstrings pulled by waves untamed,
Siren songs and salty air,
Love and longing everywhere.

Moon's reflection on the tide,
Ebb and flow with time abide,
Seagulls glide on wings so free,
Heartstrings play a melody.

Footprints trailing in the sand,
Memories held in my hand,
Waves erase but not the heart,
Bond so deep, it'll never part.

Sunset hues blend sky and sea,
Sparkling with tranquility,
Every ripple speaks to me,
Stories of eternity.

Whispers carry through the breeze,
Heartstrings playing symphonies,
Love and ocean intertwined,
A timeless dance in heart and mind.

Guardian of the Tides

Standing tall beside the shore,
Lighthouse guiding evermore,
Guardian of the restless tides,
Safe passage through the night provides.

Beacon flashing through the night,
Piercing through the fog so white,
Mariners on journeys wide,
Find their way with steadfast guide.

Waves crash with relentless might,
But the lighthouse stands upright,
Storms may rage and waters churn,
Guardian's light will ever burn.

Lonely keeper in the tower,
Watching through each passing hour,
Sacred duty, never tire,
Beacon burns with undying fire.

Silent watch through ages long,
Lighthouse standing firm and strong,
Guardian of the shifting sea,
Keeper of the tides, wild and free.

Eternal Shoreline

Endless waves caress the shore,
Rhythms of the ocean's roar,
Where the sea meets golden sand,
Whispers of a timeless land.

Ancient shells beneath my feet,
Songs of time in rhythms sweet,
Waves that kiss the distant sky,
Echoes of eternity sigh.

Tides that dance with moon's command,
Etching stories in the sand,
Windswept dunes and seagrass sway,
Painting scenes of night and day.

Children's laughter, seabird's cry,
Memories of days gone by,
Footprints left then washed away,
Ephemeral yet here to stay.

Stretches of an endless line,
Eternal shore, forever mine,
Bound by sea and sky so wide,
Nature's art in seamless tide.

Rippled Generosity

In the morning light, a river bends,
Carrying whispers, the spirit sends.
With gentle waves, it gives and mends,
A rippled journey, that never ends.

Pebbles dance in waters clear,
Nature's gift, both far and near.
The heart of giving, always sincere,
Echoes loud, for all to hear.

Through each bend, and every sway,
Generosity flows, night and day.
Silent blessings, along the way,
Ripples spread, come what may.

In the current, wisdom found,
Love and kindness, so profound.
Nature's song, a soothing sound,
Rivers of giving, all around.

So wander on, through life's terrain,
In kindness, find your refrain.
Ripples of joy, and gentle rain,
Generous hearts, forever remain.

Beyond the Briny Deep

In the depths where mermaids sleep,
Lies a world, profound and deep.
Mysteries in currents sweep,
Secrets the ocean, promises to keep.

Whales sing songs, so old and wise,
Hidden treasures beneath the skies.
Dancing shadows, nature's guise,
In the briny deep, where magic lies.

Coral castles, a sight to behold,
Stories of old, in colors bold.
Legends whispered, secrets told,
Beyond the deep, wonders unfold.

Waves caress the sandy shore,
Endless tales, forevermore.
In the ocean's timeless lore,
Adventure awaits, always in store.

So dive in deep, with heart so brave,
In the mysteries, let your soul bathe.
Discover worlds beneath the wave,
Beyond the deep, where dreams engrave.

Aquatic Benevolence

Gentle ripples, softly gleam,
Nature's touch, like a dream.
In the water's gentle stream,
Flows a kindness, serene it seems.

Fish dance in harmonic grace,
In their realm, a peaceful place.
Each reflects a calming pace,
Benevolence in liquid space.

Tides of mercy, ebb and flow,
Where compassion's rivers go.
In their depths, a subtle glow,
Aquatic peace, a gentle show.

Life beneath, in colors bright,
Shares a song of pure delight.
In their world, free from fright,
Kindness blooms, in water's light.

So cherish waves, and calm seas,
In their dance, find your ease.
Aquatic gifts, with gentle breeze,
Benevolent hearts, nature's keys.

Hands that Heal

With a touch, so soft and bright,
Hands bring comfort, in the night.
Healing words, a guiding light,
Hands that heal, hold the sight.

In every gesture, love cascades,
Soothing fears, sorrow fades.
Through their warmth, hope invades,
Kindness in each, pure parades.

Mending wounds, with tender care,
Lifting spirits, in despair.
Healing hands, always there,
In their grace, life's repairs.

Every touch, a silent prayer,
In their hold, burdens share.
Through their strength, love to bear,
Healing hearts, everywhere.

So find the hands, that softly heal,
In their touch, true love reveal.
In their warmth, life can feel,
Hands that heal, forever real.

Stardust on the Shore

Whispers of a cosmic dance,
In moonlit waves, they find their chance.
Stars fall gently on the sand,
A glow so soft, as if it's planned.

Twilight's fingers brush the tide,
Where earth and heaven coincide.
In stardust dreams, we wander free,
Caught between the sky and sea.

Underneath the velvet night,
Oceans borrow heaven's light.
Phantom whispers, ancient lore,
Stardust softly strokes the shore.

With each wave, a tale untold,
Echoes of the brave and bold.
Cosmic freckles on the earth,
Mark the sky's unending mirth.

In this dance of night and day,
Secrets in the stardust lay.
Eternal whispers on the breeze,
Time and space at last appease.

Maritime Mercy

Beneath the waves, a quiet grace,
A hidden world, a tender place.
Mercy flows in currents deep,
Where sea and silence softly seep.

Echoes hum through azure halls,
Where light in liquid patterns falls.
Life, it blooms in every hue,
In the depths so cold and true.

Shipwreck bones and coral reefs,
Hold the tales of sailors' griefs.
Yet within this ocean's heart,
Mercy threads through every part.

Tides will come and tides will go,
In their ebb, a mercy show.
Healing wounds the storms have torn,
In the sea, new hope is born.

Nodes of life in brine's embrace,
Forgiving all without a trace.
Maritime mercy, soft and grand,
Cradles gently in its hand.

Tide-Touched Redemption

Waves erode the jagged flaws,
Smoothing edges, healing cause.
In tide's embrace, a chance to mend,
A cycle that will never end.

Pain and sorrow washed away,
By the sea's persistent sway.
Nautical arms reach out in grace,
Transforming all they gently pace.

Each ripple brings a new release,
From life's chaos, brings a peace.
Salt and brine, the cleansing blend,
In oceans' arms, old wounds transcend.

Sand beneath, the footprints fade,
Of journeys past, of prayers made.
Tide-touched paths of pure revival,
Offer moments of survival.

Redemption found where waters blend,
In tide's caress, our spirits mend.
A dance of waves, that rhythm shows,
The endless cycle, life bestows.

Sunset's Gentle Hands

A canvas painted gold and red,
Softly brushed where day has bled.
Sunset's hands, they draw the line,
Between the dusk and day's decline.

Horizon whispers, evening's song,
A transition, soft yet strong.
Light diffuses, shadows play,
Final hues of waning day.

The sky's embrace of twilight's kiss,
A tender touch, a fleeting bliss.
In the arms of fading light,
Day surrenders to the night.

Stars emerge where sun once shined,
Glimmering threads, so intertwined.
Sunset's hands, they seal the pact,
Of night and day in subtle act.

Moments still in amber hue,
Day's farewell, a gentle cue.
With a touch as soft as sand,
Night unfolds by sunset's hand.

Starry Echoes of Mercy

Beneath the canvas of the night,
Stars whisper secrets, pure and bright.
Soft murmurs in the twilight glow,
A cosmic dance we yearn to know.

The moonlight weaves a gentle tale,
Of dreams adrift on a silver sail.
Guiding souls through darkest fears,
With mercy's gentle, silent tears.

In the vast abyss, a star will call,
Echoes of mercy, over all.
Hearts will listen to the gleam,
In starlight's soft, eternal dream.

Each constellation, a story feeds,
Of kindness sown like precious seeds.
Across the sky, the echoes fly,
Of mercy's song that never dies.

In the night's embrace, we find our way,
Through starry whispers night and day.
And every star, a kindred flame,
Reminds us all, we're all the same.

Coastal Crusade

Beneath the sky's azure parade,
Waves embark on a coastal crusade.
Foam and salt on sandy shore,
A timeless rhythm, forever more.

Gulls cry out above the surf,
Songs of freedom, ancient birth.
Their wings aloft in endless flight,
Guide us through the day and night.

Ships embark on quests unknown,
Through seas they've always known as home.
A crusade against the odds and storm,
In the ocean's cradle, safe and warm.

Rocks stand sentinel, timeless guards,
Witnesses to the voyaging bards.
Their tales etched on nature's skin,
Of where they've been and what they've seen.

In every wave, a whispered dare,
To journey forth, to dream, to care.
The coastal crusade calls us all,
Heed its whisper, hear its call.

Tidal Acts of Grace

Waves rise and fall in graceful dance,
A rhythmic pulse, a kind romance.
Gentle hands of ocean blue,
Caress the world, old and new.

In the ebb and flow, a story old,
Of tides that nurture, brave and bold.
They hold the secrets of the deep,
In solemn vows, forever keep.

Each crest a surge of hope and might,
They turn the dark to morning light.
Acts of grace from sea to shore,
In endless cycles, ever more.

Tidal whispers on moonlit tides,
Speak of journeys far and wide.
Carrying dreams on liquid paths,
To hearts adrift in gentle baths.

Through storms and calm, in equal stride,
The sea's embrace, a humble guide.
Such are the acts of grace we find,
In every wave, in every tide.

Seaside Redemption

Beneath the sun's golden thrall,
The seaside whispers to us all.
A place where souls can find release,
In nature's arms, in quiet peace.

Footprints left upon the sand,
A tale of journeys, hand in hand.
Each step a path to something more,
To find redemption on the shore.

The waves they cleanse, they wash away,
The burdens heavy from our day.
In saline gift, the soul renews,
In ocean's breath, we find our truths.

The salt and air, a healing balm,
To restless hearts, a welcome calm.
In every sunset's warm embrace,
We find the light of saving grace.

Upon the shore, we are reborn,
In tides of dusk, in waves of morn.
The seaside's call, a gentle mend,
A journey's start, a healing end.

Rescue at Dawn

In twilight's grip, where shadows yawn,
A sailboat drifts as night withdraws.
The sun appears, a fleeting pawn,
To guide its way with gentle laws.

Beneath the sky of pink and gold,
Waves whisper tales of journeys past.
A beacon shines, as tales unfold,
Hope stirs within the hearts at last.

Through churning seas, the vessel fights,
Against the tide's relentless push.
Then gleams a light, in dawning lights,
A savior's hand from morning's bush.

The grip of night begins to fade,
The shadows flee from solar might.
In loving arms, the crew is stayed,
Rescued at dawn from endless night.

Eternal thanks in quiet refrain,
Echo through the breaking day.
In safety's arms, no longer in pain,
The sea yields calm, as worries sway.

Shoreline Altruism

Waves kiss the shore with gentle grace,
Each rhythm sings a selfless tune.
Sand dunes bow with humble face,
Underneath the silver moon.

The fishermen with calloused hands,
Share their catch with those in need.
Where kindness flows like ocean sands,
In hearts, compassion plants its seed.

Beneath the lighthouse, children play,
Innocence wrapped in salt-tinged air.
A village thrives in every way,
With hands to help, and hearts to care.

The old, the young, all come to learn,
The gifts of giving, freely shared.
As tides of life, they shift and turn,
By love and kindness, they're repaired.

In every wave that meets the land,
A promise made to lend and heal.
On shoreline's edge, where hearts expand,
True altruism stands as real.

Maritime Acts of Kindness

Through fog and storm, a beacon shines,
Guiding souls in darkest times.
Where sailors brave the harsh confines,
Acts of kindness mark their chimes.

A lifeboat rows to save the lost,
Through icy waves and peril's fear.
Though giving might incur a cost,
Compassions' gifts bring solace near.

The harbor master, watchful, stands,
Extends a home to wandering souls.
Where weathered planks meet weathered hands,
A galleon of goodwill rolls.

Strangers greet with open hearts,
Sharing stories, warmth, and bread.
In every port, goodwill imparts,
A glow where once was only dread.

Through maritime paths we roam,
With every knot, the heart's refrain.
Acts of kindness, tide-like foam,
Leave trails of light in ocean's lane.

Ocean's Small Mercies

The sun dips low, the sky a blaze,
Where ocean meets the evening's hem.
Beyond the horizon, light delays,
And stars emerge, like precious gems.

The fisherman casts out his net,
With hopes that swim in moonlit waves.
In every catch, no offering set,
Only the ocean's gift, he saves.

A sailor lost, on tempest's ride,
Finds rest upon a driftwood spar.
In mercy's arms, where tides abide,
To guide him by a distant star.

Upon the deck the lanterns glow,
Lighting paths for those who seek.
In darkest night, soft winds bestow,
Mercies small, yet never weak.

As dawn breaks forth, the night gives way,
The ocean whispers gentle thanks.
For every soul cast where they may,
Finds mercy still in ocean's pranks.

Ocean's Benevolent Embrace

Waves whisper secrets of yore,
Soft lullabies they tenderly sing.
Cradling the shore evermore,
A tranquil, eternal spring.

Seagulls dance on sapphire hues,
Oceans hold them in gentle grace.
Whispers of tales they muse,
In this boundless, serene place.

Sunlight gleams in liquid gold,
Shimmering across the waves.
Stories of old unfold,
In the depths of hidden caves.

The vast horizon so grand,
Endless, free, they converge.
Nature's own orchestral band,
In each rise and gentle surge.

The ocean's embrace, so vast,
A mystic, boundless expanse.
Echoes of the distant past,
In its perpetual dance.

Beneath a Moonlit Canopy

Silver beams through leaves do weave,
Soft whispers in the night.
The canopy bids eve a reprieve,
Beneath the moon's soft light.

Stars twinkle in a silken sky,
A gentle, radiant sea.
Silent fireflies flit and fly,
In this nocturnal spree.

Shadows dance on emerald fields,
Nature's quiet ballet.
The night its tranquil quiet yields,
To the creatures' gentle play.

Zephyrs sing a lullaby,
Leaves rustle in reply.
As the moon watches from on high,
In her watchful, silver eye.

Dreams are woven in night's embrace,
With threads of starry light.
Beneath the canopy's ethereal grace,
In the heart of the endless night.

Sand-Scripted Sanctity

Footprints on the golden sand,
Stories etched in fleeting marks.
Nature's scripture, softly planned,
In the daylight and the dark.

Winds whisper secrets to the shore,
Songs of tides and distant lands.
Timeless echoes evermore,
In the shifting, tender sands.

Shells and pebbles find their place,
Patterns of the ocean's hand.
A mosaic in nature's grace,
On this broad, untamed land.

The sun's embrace warms the earth,
A golden kiss upon the face.
A quiet prayer, a gentle mirth,
In this serene, sacred space.

Sand scripts stories of the past,
In whispers soft and grand.
A connection sure to last,
In the heart of the boundless sand.

Rippling Benevolence

In waters crystal clear,
Ripples dance in light.
A tranquil, gentle frontier,
In the soft embrace of night.

Reflections of the sky above,
Mirror on the surface sheen.
A tender, aquatic love,
In a palette of serene.

Leaves afloat on gentle waves,
Whisper tales to the shore.
In this world that nature paves,
Peace lingers evermore.

Stars above and waves below,
In a rhythmic, silent trance.
A symphony in twilight's glow,
In a benevolent dance.

Ripples sing their soft refrain,
In a language pure and free.
Beneath the moon's tender gain,
In nature's gentle decree.

Benevolence on the Beach

Beneath the golden sun's embrace,
Waves whisper tales of time and grace.
Each footprint softly meets the shore,
A dance of kindness, evermore.

Seagulls trace their paths above,
In skies that echo waves of love.
Pebbles glisten, gems of light,
Beneath the azure skies so bright.

Children play with hearts so free,
Their laughter mingles with the sea.
Sandcastles rise with care and pride,
Built with friendship, side by side.

The ocean's song, a gentle call,
Invites compassion to us all.
With every wave that meets the strand,
We share our hearts, hand in hand.

As twilight paints the skies in hues,
Of purples, pinks, and golden blues,
A sense of peace within us spreads,
Benevolence upon us sheds.

Celestial Tides

Moonbeams dance on ocean's night,
Silver whispers soft and light.
Stars adorn a velvet sky,
As tides kiss shores with gentle sigh.

Galaxies in water's mirror,
Reflect a cosmos ever clearer.
Celestial tides in ebb and flow,
Guide the dreams that depths bestow.

Night's embrace, a tranquil song,
In harmony the worlds belong.
Each wave a story, old yet new,
Of moonlit paths the sea pursues.

Planets twinkle from afar,
Greeting waves just where they are.
The dance of time upon the sands,
Linking skies and ocean lands.

Serenades of starry light,
Blend with tides in the still of night.
Echoes of the universe,
In each wave, a tender verse.

One Shell at a Time

Along the shore, where waves embrace,
I find small treasures in their place.
Tiny shells with colors bright,
Glimmering in morning light.

Step by step, I walk with care,
Nature's gifts are everywhere.
Each shell a piece of history,
A fragment of the deep blue sea.

In my hand, I hold them tight,
Memories of ocean's sight.
One by one, they tell their tale,
Of swirling currents, mighty gales.

Oceans vast and lands afar,
Meet in shells with tales bizarre.
Through the sands, I glean a story,
Of ancient seas and their glory.

In these shells, a world confined,
Eternal bonds with life entwined.
Walking by the gentle brine,
I collect dreams, one shell at a time.